MW00584336

A HANDWRITTEN LEGACY

GRANDPA'S STORY

A MEMORY AND KEEPSAKE JOURNAL
FOR MY FAMILY

Also by Korie Herold

As You Grow : A Modern Memory Book for Baby
As We Grow : A Modern Memory Book for Married Couples
Our Christmas Story : A Modern Christmas Memory Book
Growing You : A Keepsake Pregnancy Journal
Growing Up : A Modern Memory Book for the School Years
Around Our Table : A Modern Heirloom Recipe Book
Grandma's Story : A Memory and Keepsake Journal For My Family
More Than Gratitude : 100 Days of Cultivating Deep Roots of
   Gratitude Through Guided Journaling, Prayer, & Scripture

Grandpa's Story : A Memory and Keepsake Journal For My Family
Copyright © Korie Herold
Published in 2021 by Blue Star Press
Paige Tate & Co. is an imprint of Blue Star Press
PO Box 8835, Bend, OR 97708
contact@paigetate.com | www.paigetate.com

Illustrations and Design by Korie Herold

ISBN: 9781950968572
Printed in China
10 9 8 7 6 5 4 3 2 1

This journal is dedicated to :

INTRODUCTION

This is the book I wish I had about 15 years ago. I wouldn't have hesitated to give one to my grandfather to fill in for us when he was alive and well. I can still hear his laughter in my head, but I was too young to dig deep and ask him some of the questions in this book that I'd love to hear how he would have answered.

I'm glad I am creating this now so that I can give it to my dad. My father is such an intergral part of my life, and of my children's lives. I have morning coffee with my dad just about every weekday between school drop-offs, and it really starts my day off right. We get to connect in a way that is so incredibly special, and I wish this was normal for more people. Even as much as we get together and talk, I wouldn't know half the answers to what is inside this book. That's why I think the act of filling in this book is so valuable.

This book will be his written legacy, and I already can't wait to read it. I know it will be a treasure for my boys as well, as they grow up and learn all about their grandfather.

This book is *your* written legacy.

I want your life story to live on in a meaningful way, which is why I created this keepsake book for you. My hope is that this will be a special space where you can dive into your story, pour out your heart, and pass your values and memories on to the people you love.

There are many ways you can record your story these days, but what I love about doing it in a physical book is that you get to write your memories by hand. I love handwriting—neat handwriting, messy handwriting, methodical handwriting, all of it. Handwriting is like a thumbprint that is unique to each person. I think personal storytelling is much more powerful when you get to read words that a person wrote down by hand. It means they were holding the book as they were writing in it. Their marks are now in your hands. I know you feel the difference, and I'm guessing that's why you selected this book.

A tip as you get started : Don't try to fill this book out all at once. Take your time and enjoy the process. Make yourself some tea or coffee, and settle in to tell your story on these pages. I can't stress enough that this process is meant to be enjoyed by you, the storyteller. If writing ever becomes overwhelming, simply set this book aside and come back to it later with fresh eyes. Your family will be forever grateful that you took the time to do this.

So, go ahead. You have full permission to share your thoughts and story in a way only you can do. Get to it!

Cheerfully,
Korie Herold

I would love to see *Grandpa's Story* in your hands. Use #GrandpasStory and tag @korieherold to connect on social media.

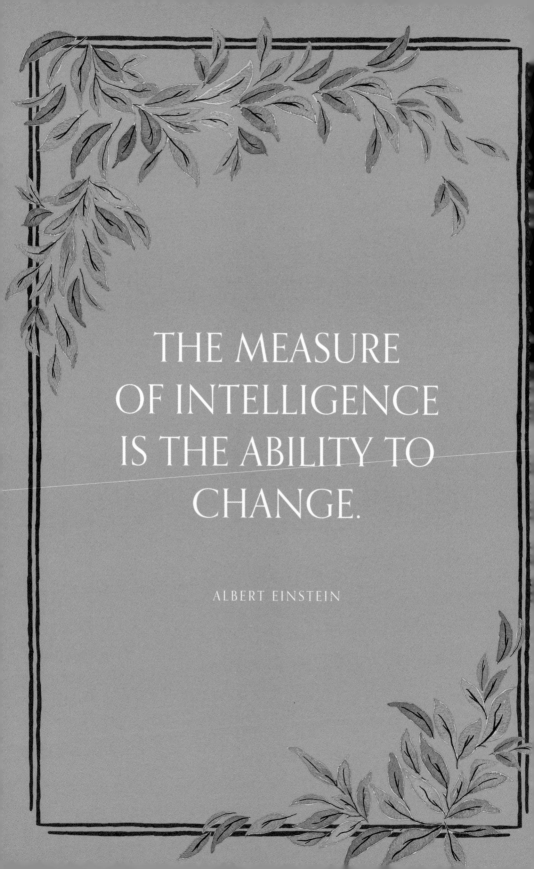

THE MEASURE
OF INTELLIGENCE
IS THE ABILITY TO
CHANGE.

ALBERT EINSTEIN

CHAPTER ONE

Early Childhood

MY FULL NAME : ....

THE STORY BEHIND MY NAME : ....

....

....

....

....

....

....

....

....

....

....

....

MY NICKNAMES GROWING UP : ....

....

....

....

MY BIRTHDAY : ....

WHERE I WAS BORN : ....

I was born in Homestead, Fla at
my grand parent home. Grandpa was
a medical doctor. After a week
mom brought me to Jupiter Fla.
The home was isolated so
it was basically Mom & Dad.

HOW I'D DESCRIBE MY PARENTS : _____

_____

_____

_____

_____

_____

_____

_____

_____

_____

_____

_____

_____

_____

_____

_____

_____

_____

_____

_____

WHAT THEY DID FOR A LIVING : _____

_____

_____

_____

_____

_____

_____

HOW I'D DESCRIBE MY GRANDPARENTS : _____

_____

_____

_____

_____

_____

_____

_____

_____

_____

_____

_____

_____

_____

_____

_____

_____

_____

_____

_____

WHAT THEY DID FOR A LIVING : _____

_____

_____

_____

_____

_____

HERE'S WHAT OUR HOUSE WAS LIKE GROWING UP :

THIS IS WHO I PLAYED WITH THE MOST GROWING UP : _____

_____

_____

_____

_____

_____

_____

_____

_____

_____

_____

MY FAVORITE TOYS OR PLAYTIME ACTIVITIES : _____

_____

_____

_____

_____

_____

HOW I'D DESCRIBE MY CHILDHOOD BEDROOM : _____

_____

_____

_____

_____

FAMILY MEALTIME AS A CHILD WAS LIKE THIS :

MY PETS GROWING UP :

MY FAVORITE EARLY CHILDHOOD MEMORY :

WHAT I MISS MOST ABOUT BEING A CHILD :

ADD PHOTO

ADDITIONAL THOUGHTS OR STORIES ABOUT MY EARLY CHILDHOOD : _____

CHAPTER TWO

The School Years

MY FRIENDS IN SCHOOL : _____

_____

_____

_____

_____

_____

_____

MY FAVORITE SCHOOL SUBJECT : _____

_____

ACTIVITIES, SPORTS, OR CLUBS I WAS INVOLVED IN : _____

_____

_____

_____

_____

WHAT I ENJOYED DOING OUTSIDE OF SCHOOL : _____

_____

_____

_____

_____

_____

MY FAVORITE MUSIC, TV SHOWS, AND BOOKS GROWING UP :

_____

_____

_____

_____

_____

HOW I'D DESCRIBE MYSELF AS A TEENAGER :

_____

_____

_____

_____

_____

_____

_____

_____

_____

_____

WHAT I THOUGHT I WANTED TO BE WHEN I GREW UP :

_____

_____

_____

_____

_____

_____

_____

A MEMORABLE TIME I GOT IN TROUBLE : _____

MY FAVORITE HIGH SCHOOL MEMORY :

MY FAVORITE TEACHER/COACH, AND WHAT MADE THEM SO GREAT :

WHAT I DID AFTER HIGH SCHOOL :

WHAT I WOULD HAVE DONE DIFFERENTLY IN SCHOOL IF I HAD
THE CHANCE :

WHAT I MISS MOST ABOUT SCHOOL : _____

ADD PHOTO

ADDITIONAL THOUGHTS OR STORIES ABOUT MY TIME IN SCHOOL : _____

CHAPTER THREE

Work & Travel

MY FIRST JOB : ....

....

....

....

....

....

....

....

....

....

....

THE JOB THAT SHAPED ME THE MOST IN LIFE AND WHY : ....

....

....

....

....

....

....

....

....

....

....

....

....

....

....

MY LONGEST HELD JOB WAS :

ADVICE I'D SHARE ABOUT WORKING :

MY FIRST CAR : ....

....

....

....

....

....

....

....

THE CAR THAT CARRIES THE MOST SIGNIFICANT MEMORIES WITH IT, AND WHAT THOSE ARE :

....

....

....

....

....

....

....

....

....

....

....

....

....

....

THE FAMILY VACATIONS I HOLD DEAREST :

THE FURTHEST PLACE I'VE TRAVELED :

MY FAVORITE PLACE TO TRAVEL :

ADD PHOTO

ADDITIONAL THOUGHTS OR STORIES ABOUT WORK AND TRAVELING : ———————

CHAPTER FOUR

Love & Family

MY FIRST DATE : _____

_____

_____

_____

_____

_____

_____

_____

_____

_____

_____

_____

THE STORY OF MY FIRST KISS : _____

_____

_____

_____

_____

_____

_____

_____

_____

_____

_____

_____

_____

_____

THE MOST ROMANTIC MOMENT OF MY LIFE :

HOW I MET YOUR GRANDMOTHER : _____

_____

_____

_____

_____

_____

_____

_____

_____

_____

_____

_____

_____

_____

_____

_____

_____

_____

_____

_____

HOW LONG WE DATED BEFORE WE SETTLED DOWN : _____

_____

_____

_____

_____

_____

_____

A FAVORITE TIME OF MINE SPENT WITH YOUR GRANDMOTHER : _____

_____

_____

_____

_____

_____

_____

_____

_____

_____

_____

_____

_____

_____

_____

_____

_____

MY BEST RELATIONSHIP ADVICE : _____

_____

_____

_____

_____

_____

HOW MY CHILDREN'S NAMES WERE CHOSEN :

_____

_____

_____

_____

_____

_____

_____

_____

_____

_____

_____

HOW I'D DESCRIBE RAISING OUR FAMILY :

_____

_____

_____

_____

_____

_____

_____

_____

_____

_____

_____

_____

_____

_____

_____

THE MEAL/DISH I MOST ENJOY SHARING WITH OUR FAMILY :

_____
_____
_____
_____
_____
_____

MY FAVORITE MEMORY OF RAISING OUR FAMILY : _____

_____
_____
_____
_____
_____
_____
_____
_____
_____
_____
_____
_____
_____
_____
_____
_____

WHAT I MISS MOST ABOUT HAVING YOUNG CHILDREN IN THE HOUSE :

HOW I FELT THE DAY I FOUND OUT I WAS GOING TO BE A GRANDFATHER :

MY DEFINITION OF THE WORD "LOVE" :

ADD PHOTO

ADDITIONAL THOUGHTS OR STORIES ABOUT FAMILY & RELATIONSHIPS :

CHAPTER FIVE

Character & Values

THREE CHARACTERISTICS ABOUT MYSELF THAT I VALUE :

HOW PEOPLE WHO KNOW ME WELL WOULD DESCRIBE ME:

THREE TRAITS I VALUE IN MY FRIENDS AND FAMILY, OR WHEN MAKING NEW RELATIONSHIPS :

A COMPLIMENT SOMEONE GAVE ME THAT I WILL
NEVER FORGET:

THE BEST PIECE OF ADVICE I EVER RECEIVED :

UP TO THIS POINT, HERE'S THE ONE THING I WOULD HAVE DONE DIFFERENTLY WITH
OR IN MY LIFE :

UP TO THIS POINT, THIS IS THE MOST CHARACTER-DEFINING EVENT OF MY LIFE :

THE HARDEST THING I'VE EVER GONE THROUGH :

ONE OF MY PROUDEST MOMENTS :

MY FAVORITE QUOTE OR VERSE THAT GUIDES ME :

THE ROLE OF FAITH OR SPIRITUALITY IN MY LIFE :

THE THINGS I VALUE MOST IN LIFE :

_____

_____

_____

_____

_____

_____

_____

_____

_____

THE VALUES I HOPE TO PASS DOWN AND INSTILL IN MY FAMILY :

_____

_____

_____

_____

_____

_____

_____

_____

_____

MY FAVORITE WAY TO MAKE OTHERS FEEL LOVED/SPECIAL :

_____

_____

_____

_____

_____

_____

ADD PHOTO

ADDITIONAL THOUGHTS ON CHARACTER AND VALUES :

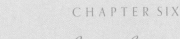

CHAPTER SIX

Hypotheticals & Curiosities

IF I COULD THROW A DINNER PARTY AND INVITE 3 OTHER PEOPLE, DEAD OR ALIVE, THIS IS WHO I WOULD INVITE AND WHY :

ONE THING I ALWAYS WISH I HAD TRIED OR EXPERIENCED :

_____
_____
_____
_____
_____
_____
_____
_____
_____
_____
_____
_____

ONE THING I THINK YOU SHOULD LEARN MORE ABOUT AND WHY IT'S WORTH IT :

_____
_____
_____
_____
_____
_____
_____
_____
_____
_____
_____
_____
_____

MY GIFTS AND TALENTS, AND HOW I'VE GOTTEN TO USE THEM IN MY LIFE :

THE BEST PURCHASE I'VE EVER MADE, AND WHAT MADE IT SO MEMORABLE :

BOOKS, MUSIC, ART, AND FILMS THAT I ENJOY :

HOW I'D DESCRIBE THE PERFECT DAY IF IT WERE UP TO ME :

MY FAVORITE WAY TO TREAT MYSELF :

ONE THING ABOUT ME THAT MAY SURPRISE YOU : _____

_____

_____

_____

_____

_____

_____

SOUNDS THAT BRING ME JOY TO HEAR : _____

_____

_____

_____

_____

_____

_____

SIMPLE THINGS IN LIFE THAT BRING ME GREAT JOY : _____

_____

_____

_____

_____

_____

_____

MY FAVORITE GAME TO PLAY :

THE MOST INTERESTING PERSON I HAVE EVER MET :

THE PERSON THAT INSPIRES ME THE MOST :

THE NATIONAL OR WORLD EVENTS THAT I REMEMBER MOST FROM MY LIFETIME :

SOMETHING I'M REALLY BAD AT NO MATTER HOW HARD I TRY :

MY PET PEEVES :

THE THREE THINGS THAT I OWN THAT MEAN THE MOST TO ME :

ADD PHOTO

ADDITIONAL THOUGHTS I'D LIKE TO SHARE ABOUT MY LIFE :

CHAPTER SEVEN

Words of Wisdom

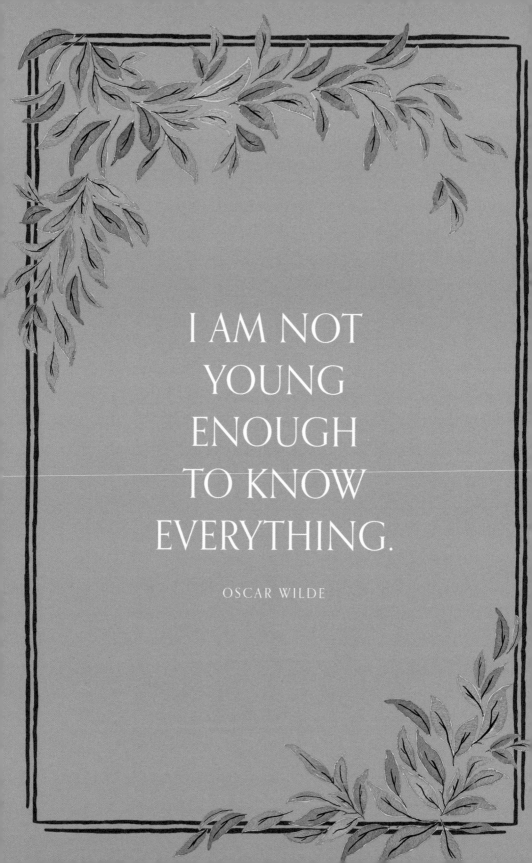

I AM NOT YOUNG ENOUGH TO KNOW EVERYTHING.

OSCAR WILDE

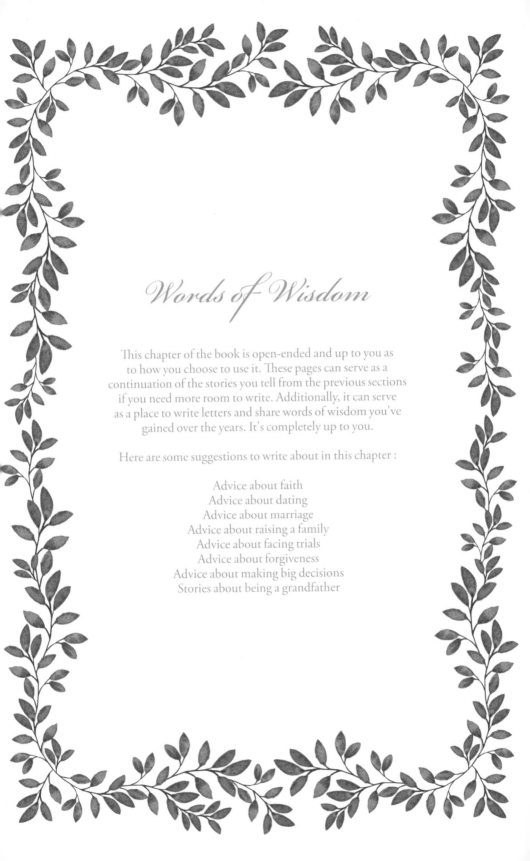

Words of Wisdom

This chapter of the book is open-ended and up to you as to how you choose to use it. These pages can serve as a continuation of the stories you tell from the previous sections if you need more room to write. Additionally, it can serve as a place to write letters and share words of wisdom you've gained over the years. It's completely up to you.

Here are some suggestions to write about in this chapter :

Advice about faith
Advice about dating
Advice about marriage
Advice about raising a family
Advice about facing trials
Advice about forgiveness
Advice about making big decisions
Stories about being a grandfather

YOUR STORIES ARE WORTH TELLING

We believe this in our core, which is why we're creating the heirloom books that we do. We believe in quality materials, timeless design, and a whole lot of heart. We invite you to visit our website to dive into any of the books in our current lineup and get a deeper look at the contents, purpose of the book, who it's for, and what makes each one special.

WWW.KORIEHEROLD.COM
for more information

OTHER GIFTABLE BOOKS BY KORIE HEROLD

GROWING YOU : A KEEPSAKE PREGNANCY JOURNAL AND MEMORY BOOK FOR MOM & BABY - *Growing You* is a place to celebrate and chronicle your pregnancy journey, reflecting on the growth, anticipation, and memories that you want to hold onto as a mother. This heirloom-quality book is designed with a timeless look and archival paper so that you can one day pass it along to your child. This journal is perfect to gift someone early on in their pregnancy.

AS YOU GROW : A MODERN MEMORY BOOK FOR BABY - A modern take on a baby memory book and journal, *As You Grow* stands out from the crowd of baby books with its elegant, chic, and timeless design. The gender-neutral artwork with guided sections provide space for your family to record moments from pregnancy to age five. It's a book you can interact with now, and look back on for a lifetime. The design promotes longevity, as this keepsake book is intended to be shared and displayed for years to come. *As You Grow* is inclusive of every modern family. This book makes a great gift for a parent at a baby shower.

GROWING UP : A MODERN MEMORY BOOK FOR THE SCHOOL YEARS - *Growing Up* is a modern memory book for the school years and features gender-neutral artwork and space to record precious memories from each year of your child's schooling so you can one day gift to your grown child. The book includes space to record moments for each grade level from kindergarten through high school.

OUR CHRISTMAS STORY : A MODERN MEMORY BOOK FOR CHRISTMAS - Cherish your favorite memories by writing down meaningful traditions, remember holiday celebrations you hosted or attended, record special gifts given or received, save photos with Santa or annual family Christmas cards, preserve treasured family holiday recipes, and so much more! This book makes for a thoughtful gift for a bridal shower, wedding gift, or for a family who loves to celebrate Christmas.

AROUND OUR TABLE : A MODERN HEIRLOOM RECIPE BOOK TO ORGANIZE AND PRESERVE YOUR FAMILY'S MOST CHERISHED MEALS - Your family's most cherished meals deserve to be remembered. Preserve all of your favorite recipes, and the memories associated with them, in this heirloom-quality blank recipe book. The book includes 7 sections to organize your recipes, blank recipe pages, 20 loose recipe cards, plastic sleeves to preserve new and old recipes, and a pocket folder in the back for additional storage.

AS WE GROW : A MODERN MEMORY BOOK FOR MARRIED COUPLES - *As We Grow* is a place to celebrate and remember the details of your marriage. Record the story of how you live and love and preserve it in writing—a treasure you can pass to your children and grandchildren. It's the perfect gift for the newly engaged couple, the newly married couple, or those who have been married for years!

WHAT PEOPLE ARE SAYING
ABOUT KORIE HEROLD BOOKS

"Korie is an artist at heart but also has an overwhelming sense of legacy to everything she does. Her other books have a way of making you pause, slow down, and memorialize a fleeting season to enjoy later." - Lauren Swann

"When you see how beautiful and detail-oriented her books are, you become a customer for life. Thank you, Korie, for thinking of everything and creating treasures that will be passed down through future generations." - Paige Frey

"The quality is unbelievable and it's such a gorgeous place to preserve all those cherished memories. And it looks beautiful on my shelf next to my other memory books from Korie! ... I love the attention to detail Korie includes in her books." - Maria Hilsenbrand

"By far, I think my favorite thing about As You Grow *is that my son will one day be able to cherish this time capsule of sorts. He'll know exactly how he was loved, thought of, and remembered as my sweet little boy."*
- Alyse Morrissey

WWW.KORIEHEROLD.COM